I LOVE YOU SO MUSH

summersdale

I LOVE YOU SO MUSH

This edition copyright © Octopus Publishing Group Limited, 2024
First published as *Olive You* in 2018

An Hachette UK Company
www.hachette.co.uk

Summersdale Publishers
Part of Octopus Publishing Group Limited
Carmelite House
50 Victoria Embankment
LONDON
EC4Y 0DZ
UK

www.summersdale.com

Printed and bound in China

ISBN: 978-1-83799-447-2

This FSC® label means that materials used for the product have been responsibly sourced

MIX
Paper | Supporting
responsible forestry
FSC® C016973

Substantial discounts on bulk quantities of Summersdale books are available to corporations, professional associations and other organizations. For details contact general enquiries: telephone: +44 (0) 1243 771107 or email: enquiries@summersdale.com.

To...

From...

I LOVE YOU

A LATTE

IN ALL THE
WORLD THERE
IS NO **HEART**
FOR ME LIKE
YOURS.

Maya Angelou

IT JUST SORT OF
HAPPENED,
IN THE WAY THAT
LOVE OFTEN
DOES: NATURALLY,
INSTINCTUALLY AND
WHOLEHEARTEDLY.

Jodi Picoult

Love is the
ANSWER
to everything.
It's the only
REASON
to do anything.

Ray Bradbury

WITH A
KISS
LET US SET
OUT FOR AN
UNKNOWN
WORLD.

Alfred de Musset

LOVE

is the one
wild card.

Taylor Swift

YOU MAKE MY
HEART

SKIP A BEET

Love is like a precious PLANT...
You've got to really look after it.

John Lennon

LOVE IS
QUIVERING
HAPPINESS.

Kahlil Gibran

YOU ARE
JUST

MY TYPE

Lovers alone wear

SUNLIGHT.

E. E. Cummings

IF YOU LOVE
SOMEONE, YOU
WANT TO
TREAT THEM,
SURPRISE THEM,
REMIND THEM
HOW YOU FEEL.

David Beckham

BEING DEEPLY
LOVED BY
SOMEONE GIVES
YOU **STRENGTH**,
WHILE LOVING
SOMEONE DEEPLY
GIVES YOU
COURAGE.

Anonymous

I DONUT KNOW
WHAT I'D DO

WITHOUT YOU

I have been
LOVING
you a little more
every minute
since this
MORNING.

Victor Hugo

ALL LOVE
STORIES ARE
TALES OF
BEGINNINGS.

Meghan O'Rourke

YOU LIGHT UP

MY LIFE

TILL IT HAS **LOVED** – NO **MAN** OR **WOMAN** CAN BECOME ITSELF.

Emily Dickinson

I THINK YOU CAN LIVE **ANYWHERE** AND DO **ANYTHING** WHEN YOU'RE CRAZY IN **LOVE.**

Nicole Kidman

In the harshest
place on Earth,
love finds a
WAY.

Morgan Freeman

YOU ARE ALL

I'VE AVO
WANTED

You are my heart,
my life,
my one and only
THOUGHT.

Arthur Conan Doyle

I THINK
ROMANCE
BASICALLY
STARTS WITH
RESPECT.

Bill Murray

I

WHALEY

LOVE YOU

I love you with
so much of my

HEART

that none is
left to protest.

William Shakespeare

WHAT IS THE
BEGINNING?
LOVE.
WHAT THE
COURSE?
LOVE STILL.

Christina Rossetti

THE BEST
AND MOST
BEAUTIFUL
THINGS IN THE
WORLD CANNOT
BE SEEN OR
EVEN TOUCHED.
THEY MUST BE FELT
WITH THE HEART.

Helen Keller

WE ARE THE

PERFECT PEAR

LOVE,

and do what thou wilt.

St Augustine of Hippo

I LOVE **LOVE**,
I LOVE BEING
IN LOVE. IT'S
AMAZING
AND SO **FUN**.

Rita Ora

I WANNA

PIZZA YOU

IT IS EASILY
THE MOST EMPTY
CLICHÉ, THE
MOST USELESS
WORD, AND AT
THE SAME TIME THE
MOST POWERFUL
HUMAN EMOTION.

Toni Morrison on love

LOVE IS **COMPOSED** OF A SINGLE SOUL INHABITING **TWO BODIES.**

Aristotle

Just in case
you ever
foolishly forget;
I'm never not
THINKING
OF YOU.

Virginia Woolf

I WANT TO BEE

WITH YOU
FOREVER

We loved
with a love
that was
more than
LOVE.

Edgar Allan Poe

THERE IS ONLY
ONE HAPPINESS
IN LIFE, **TO LOVE**
AND **BE LOVED**.

George Sand

I LOVE YOU
FROM MY HEAD

TO-MA-TOES

LOVE
unlocks doors
and opens
windows that
weren't even
there before.

Mignon McLaughlin

LOVE MUST
BE AS MUCH
A LIGHT
AS IT IS
A FLAME.

Henry David Thoreau

ROMANCE
IS THE GLAMOUR
WHICH TURNS
THE DUST OF
EVERYDAY
LIFE INTO A
GOLDEN HAZE.

Elinor Glyn

YOU SWEEP ME

OFF MY FEET

In dreams
and in
LOVE
there are no
impossibilities.

János Arany

THERE IS NO
GREATER SOURCE
OF **JOY** AND
MEANING IN OUR
LIVES THAN OUR
RELATIONSHIPS
WITH OTHERS.

Esther Perel

YOU ARE ONE

IN A MELON

THE CHANCE
TO **LOVE** AND BE
LOVED EXISTS NO
MATTER WHERE
YOU ARE.

Oprah Winfrey

FOR YOU SEE,
EACH DAY I LOVE
YOU **MORE**,
TODAY MORE
THAN YESTERDAY
AND LESS THAN
TOMORROW.

Rosemonde Gérard

ROMANCE

is thinking about your significant other, when you are supposed to be

THINKING

about something else.

Nicholas Sparks

TIME FRIES WHEN

I AM WITH YOU

There's no bad
consequence
to loving

FULLY,

with all your
heart.

Reese Witherspoon

WHO WOULD GIVE
A LAW TO LOVERS?
LOVE IS UNTO ITSELF
A HIGHER LAW.

Boethius

YOU ARE
OTTERLY

AMAZING

When you
LOVE
someone that much,
even if something
comes between you,
it's a love that
NEVER
really dies.

Justin Bieber

INDEED,
THE **IDEAL** STORY
IS THAT OF TWO
PEOPLE WHO GO
INTO **LOVE** STEP
FOR STEP.

Robert Louis Stevenson

THE **BEST** THING
TO HOLD ON
TO IN LIFE IS
EACH OTHER.

Audrey Hepburn

YOU ARE SUCH A

CUTE-CUMBER

Love grows more
TREMENDOUSLY
full, swift, poignant,
as the years
MULTIPLY.

Zane Grey

WHO,
BEING **LOVED**,
IS POOR?

Oscar Wilde

YOU BLOW

ME AWAY

I LOOK AT
YOU AND SEE
THE REST OF MY
LIFE IN FRONT
OF MY EYES.

Anonymous

THERE IS NO INSTINCT LIKE THAT OF THE **HEART.**

Lord Byron

I saw that you were

PERFECT,

and so I loved you.
Then I saw that you
were not perfect
and I loved you
even more.

Angelita Lim

I BE-LEAF

IN YOU

Love is something eternal; the ASPECT may change, but not the ESSENCE.

Vincent van Gogh

I HAVE LOVED
NONE BUT
YOU.

Jane Austen

I AM WEIGH

INTO YOU

I say of Love
that he is the
fairest and best in
himself, and the
cause of what is

FAIREST

and best in all
other things.

Plato

THE HEART THAT LOVES IS **ALWAYS YOUNG**.

Greek proverb

WE LOVE
BECAUSE IT'S
THE ONLY TRUE
ADVENTURE.

Nikki Giovanni

YOU HAVE

NICE BUNS

MORNING

without you is
a dwindled
dawn.

Emily Dickinson

LOVE... YOU
THRILLING,
SPINE-TINGLING,
INTOXICATING,
LIFE-CHANGING,
AWAKENING
FEELING. I'M
READY FOR YOU,
ALWAYS!

Fearne Cotton

OUR KETCHUPS

ARE THE BEST

I LOVE YOU
NOT ONLY FOR
WHAT YOU ARE,
BUT FOR WHAT I AM
WHEN I AM
WITH YOU.

Mary Carolyn Davies

I KNOW BY
EXPERIENCE
THAT THE POETS
ARE RIGHT:
LOVE IS
ETERNAL.

E. M. Forster

Love isn't
something you
FIND.
Love is something
that finds you.

Loretta Young

YOU ARE

A HOOT

You get to
CHOOSE
who you love and
who you give your
heart to.

Emma Watson

YOU HAVE
MY WHOLE
HEART FOR MY
WHOLE LIFE.

French proverb

I LOVE YOU
TOOTH THE MOON

AND BACK

To love
is to find
PLEASURE
in the happiness
of others.

Gottfried Wilhelm Leibniz

WHEN YOU
LOVE SOMEONE
ALL YOUR
SAVED-UP
WISHES START
COMING OUT.

Elizabeth Bowen

LOVE!
LOVE UNTIL
THE NIGHT
COLLAPSES!

Pablo Neruda

YOU MAKE ME

SO HA-PEA

Love is like a tree;
it sprouts forth
of itself, sends its
roots out deeply
through our whole
BEING.

Victor Hugo

LOVE IS
SHARING YOUR
POPCORN.

Charles M. Schulz

IT MUSTARD

BE LOVE

TO GET
THE FULL VALUE
OF A **JOY**
YOU MUST HAVE
SOMEBODY
TO **DIVIDE**
IT WITH.

Mark Twain

IF WE ARE **BOLD**, LOVE STRIKES AWAY THE CHAINS OF FEAR FROM OUR **SOULS**.

Maya Angelou

To love and win
is the best thing.
To love and lose
is the next
BEST.

William Makepeace Thackeray

YOU ROCK

MY WORLD

You don't find
LOVE;
it
FINDS
YOU.

Anaïs Nin

IT'S ALWAYS
WRONG TO
HATE, BUT IT'S
NEVER WRONG
TO LOVE.

Lady Gaga

I FIND
YOU VERY

APPEELING

LOVE
is the whole
and more
than all.

E. E. Cummings

HOW ON EARTH
ARE YOU EVER
GOING TO
EXPLAIN IN TERMS
OF **CHEMISTRY**
AND PHYSICS SO
IMPORTANT A
BIOLOGICAL
PHENOMENON
AS FIRST LOVE?

Albert Einstein

TO THE **WORLD**
YOU MAY JUST BE
ONE PERSON, BUT
TO ONE PERSON
YOU MAY BE THE
WORLD.

Anonymous

TO ME, YOU ARE

PURR-FECT

Love needs
no publicity
because love
JUST IS.

Prince

EACH TIME
YOU **HAPPEN** TO
ME ALL OVER
AGAIN.

Edith Wharton

YOU ARE MY

ANCHOR

A KISS
MAKES THE
HEART **YOUNG**
AGAIN AND WIPES
OUT THE YEARS.

Rupert Brooke

MY
HEART HAS
MADE ITS MIND
UP AND I'M
AFRAID IT'S
YOU.

Wendy Cope

Love is
most nearly itself
When here and
now cease to
MATTER.

T. S. Eliot

I LOVE EWE

SO MUCH

I ask you to pass
through life at
MY SIDE —
to be my
second self, and
best earthly
COMPANION.

Charlotte Brontë

IF I KNOW
WHAT **LOVE IS**,
IT IS BECAUSE
OF **YOU**.

Hermann Hesse

YOU ARE

GRAPE

LOVE

does not dominate; it

CULTIVATES.

And that is more.

Johann Wolfgang von Goethe

MY
HEART
IS LIKE A
SINGING
BIRD.

Christina Rossetti

IS NOT
A KISS THE VERY
AUTOGRAPH
OF LOVE?

Henry Theophilus Finck

FANCY A

SPOON?

There are
never enough
"I LOVE
YOUS".

Lenny Bruce

THE GREATEST
TREASURES ARE
THOSE INVISIBLE
TO THE EYE BUT
FOUND BY
THE HEART.

Judy Garland

YOU ARE

TEA-RRIFIC

LOVE IS LIKE **SMILING**; IT NEVER FADES AND IS **CONTAGIOUS.**

Paula Deen

THE ONE **THING** WE CAN NEVER GET ENOUGH OF IS LOVE.

Henry Miller

Love

LOVES

to love love.

James Joyce

WANNA

CHILL?

If you find

SOMEONE

you love in

your life, then

HANG ON

to that love.

Diana, Princess of Wales

ANYONE CAN BE
PASSIONATE,
BUT IT TAKES
REAL LOVERS
TO BE SILLY.

Rose Franken

I AM

TURTLEY

IN LOVE WITH YOU

Love is

FRIENDSHIP

that has caught

FIRE.

Ann Landers

BUT TO **SEE HER**
WAS TO LOVE HER;
LOVE BUT HER,
AND LOVE
FOREVER.

Robert Burns

I KNOW
OF ONLY
ONE DUTY,
AND THAT
IS TO **LOVE.**

Albert Camus

YOU ARE

SIZZLING

I want nothing
from love,
in short, but

LOVE.

Colette

ALL WE HAVE
TO DO IS JUST
ADMIRE EACH
OTHER AND LOVE
EACH OTHER
24 HOURS A DAY
UNTIL WE VANISH.

Yoko Ono

LOOKING

FOXY

THERE IS
NO **REMEDY**
FOR LOVE
BUT TO LOVE
MORE.

Henry David Thoreau

THERE IS
NO **CHARM**
EQUAL TO
TENDERNESS
OF HEART.

Jane Austen

Ever
THINE,
ever
MINE,
ever
OURS.

Ludwig van Beethoven

WE ARE BUTTER

TOGETHER

To love
abundantly is to live
ABUNDANTLY,
and to love
forever is to live
FOREVER.

Henry Drummond

TO BE **BRAVE** IS TO
LOVE SOMEONE
UNCONDITIONALLY,
WITHOUT EXPECTING
ANYTHING IN
RETURN.

Madonna

YOU'RE

DINO-MITE

How do I love
THEE?
Let me count
the ways.

Elizabeth Barrett Browning

WE ARE MOST **ALIVE** WHEN WE'RE IN LOVE.

John Updike

TO FALL
IN LOVE IS
TO CREATE
A **RELIGION**
THAT HAS A
FALLIBLE GOD.

Jorge Luis Borges

I AM NUTS

ABOUT YOU

Love is an
act of endless
forgiveness, a
TENDER
look which
becomes a
HABIT.

Peter Ustinov

THE SOUL OF LOVE
IS THE **INVINCIBLE**
DIFFERENCE OF
LOVERS, WHILE ITS
SUBTLE MATTER IS
THE IDENTITY OF
THEIR DESIRES.

Paul Valéry

I WANNA

STICK WITH YOU

KISS ME, AND YOU WILL SEE HOW IMPORTANT I AM.

Sylvia Plath

MY CREED
IS **LOVE** AND
YOU ARE ITS
ONLY **TENET**.

John Keats

LOVE

is not love which
alters when it
alteration finds.

William Shakespeare

YOU ARE
BACON

ME CRAZY

To love is
to receive
a glimpse of
HEAVEN.

Karen Sunde

A **HEART**
SET ON LOVE
WILL **DO NO**
WRONG.

Confucius

THANK YOU
FOR BEAN

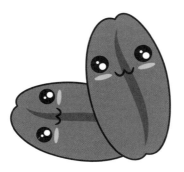

THE BEST

You
CAN'T
CHOOSE
who you fall
in love with,
you know?

Kate Winslet

YOU WILL NEVER
LEARN WHAT LOVE
IS ON ANY LEVEL
UNTIL YOU LET
SOMEONE LOVE
YOU THE WAY YOU
DESERVE TO BE
LOVED.

Kelly Osbourne

KISSING... IS THE MOST DELICIOUS, MOST BEAUTIFUL AND PASSIONATE THING THAT TWO PEOPLE CAN DO, BAR NONE.

Drew Barrymore

ALOE YOU

VERA MUCH

YET IT IS ONLY LOVE WHICH **SETS US FREE.**

Maya Angelou

I LOVE YOU

SO MUSH

Have you enjoyed this book?
If so, find us on Facebook at **Summersdale Publishers**, on Twitter/X at **@Summersdale** and on Instagram and TikTok at **@summersdalebooks** and get in touch. We'd love to hear from you!

www.summersdale.com